THE MONEY GAME

MARK HALLINK

The Money Game

© Copyright 2025, Mark Hallink

Published By: Springwell Publishing

First Edition 1-2-3-4-5-6-7-8-9-10

All Rights Reserved

Printed in the United States

ISBN (Hardback): 978-1-9717559-6-0
ISBN (Paperback): 978-1-9717559-7-7
ISBN (eBook): 979-8-9922405-2-8
ISBN (Audiobook): 979-8-9923032-2-3

Library of Congress Control Number: 2025911401

Also by Mark Halink

Pumpkin's Pennies

How To Speak To A Robot

Quiet Money

CONTENTS

Mastering the Money Game

ife isn't fair, but it's not entirely random either. The rules of money are subtle, often hidden behind marketing, societal pressures, and personal habits. Yet, they govern everything from how we earn, spend, and save, to how we find financial freedom—or don't. The problem is, that most people never realize they're playing a game, let alone that it has rules. They're too busy working, spending, and surviving to ask, "Am I winning?"

This book is your guide to seeing the game for what it is—and learning how to play it smarter.

WHY THE MONEY GAME MATTERS

Money touches every aspect of our lives. It shapes our choices, dictates our opportunities, and impacts our relationships. But here's the kicker: money isn't the goal; it's the tool. Success isn't measured by how much money you have, but by how effectively you use it to create the life you want.

A PERSONAL NOTE

When I was young, growing up likely the poorest kid in my class, I believed money was the key to happiness. It wasn't until much later, after building a business and facing countless challenges, that I realized I had been asking the wrong questions. Money wasn't the goal; it was a tool—a means to achieve freedom, security, and fulfillment.

That realization changed everything. It helped me see the hidden rules of the game and use them to my advantage. It's my hope this book will do the same for you.

WHAT YOU'LL LEARN

This isn't your typical personal finance book. Yes, we'll cover strategies for saving, investing, and growing wealth. But more importantly, we will explore the mindset, habits, and relationships that underpin financial success. Along the way, we'll tackle big questions like:

- What's the real value of money, and how does it relate to your time and energy?
- How do you set meaningful goals—and avoid the traps that come with achieving them?
- Why are the people you surround yourself with just as important as your financial choices?
- How can you adapt to chaos, entropy, and the unexpected curveballs life throws your way?

THE RULES OF THE GAME

Throughout this book, you will discover ten fundamental rules that govern the Money Game. They're simple, but not always easy. Rules like:

- If you're spending money that wasn't generated by a return on investment, you're losing the game.
- Time and energy are more valuable than money. Treat them as such.
- Surround yourself with people who align with your goals and values— they will make or break your success.

Each chapter builds on these rules, providing insights, examples, and actionable strategies to help you navigate the game on your terms.

A JOURNEY THROUGH CHAOS AND LUCK

Life is unpredictable. Chaos, entropy, and luck are constants, shaping our lives in ways we can't always control.

But here's the good news: while you can't eliminate chaos, you can learn to adapt.

While you can't manufacture luck, you can position yourself to take advantage of it when it strikes.

From personal stories of near-collapse to lessons drawn from history and science, this book will show you how to embrace uncertainty and use it as a stepping stone, not a stumbling block.

A TOUCH OF HUMOR

Money is a serious subject, but this isn't a boring textbook.

We'll laugh at the absurdities, reflect on the ironies, and find joy in the journey.

Because at the end of the day, the Money Game isn't just about winning—it's about enjoying the process.

Your Next Move... This book is your invitation to take control. To stop reacting to life and start shaping it.

To learn the rules of the game and play it to win it. So, grab a coffee (or make one at home to save $6—more on that later), and let's get started.

CHAPTER ONE

Luck, Entropy, and Chaos

Have you ever stared into the abyss?

No, not literally into some dark, bottomless pit, but into a moment in your life where you felt everything you valued was slipping away. Maybe it was a financial ruin, a devastating diagnosis, or the sudden loss of someone you loved.

It's in those moments you come to understand the true nature of luck—and how little control we sometimes have over it.

LUCK AND THE ABYSS

The abyss looks different for everyone, shaped by personal values and cultural expectations. For some, it's a total financial collapse. For others, it's the loss of health, relationships, or even reputation. Whatever form it takes, the abyss represents a moment where everything you hold dear feels at risk, and chaos threatens to take over.

If you've been there, you know how it feels. If you haven't, take a moment to imagine what your abyss might look like. Is it losing your job? Your home? A loved one? Whatever it is, one thing is certain: facing the abyss changes how you view luck.

Here's the thing about luck: it's often misunderstood. People like to say things like, "You make your own luck," and while there's some truth to that, there's also pure, unexplainable chance. Let me give you an example.

Imagine being an airline pilot mid-Atlantic when your engines fail due to a catastrophic mechanical problem.

You should crash into the ocean, but through a combination of skill and pure chance, you manage to glide the plane to a safe landing in the Azores.

That's luck. Yes, the pilot's training and skill were essential, but without a massive dose of good fortune, things could have turned out very differently.

CHAOS AND ENTROPY: THE UNIVERSE'S FAVORITE HOBBY

Before we dive deeper, let's talk about entropy. If you're not familiar, entropy is the second law of thermodynamics' way of saying, "Things fall apart, and they love doing it."

This isn't just a theory—it's a fact of life, the universe, and everything in it. Left unattended, your house will get messy, your car will rust, and your plans will go sideways. Entropy is the ultimate party crasher, always lurking, always ready to turn order into chaos.

It's why your perfectly packed suitcase explodes into a jumble of socks and shampoo bottles the moment you unzip it. It's also why, no matter how much effort you put into keeping things together, life insists on throwing curveballs your way.

APOLLO 13: A CLEAR GOAL TURNED UPSIDE DOWN

Let's look at a famous example: the Apollo 13 mission. When NASA launched the mission in 1970, there was a clear goal—to land astronauts on the moon and bring them home safely. The astronauts on board—Jim Lovell, Jack Swigert, and Fred Haise—were fully prepared to carry out this goal.

However, shortly after reaching Earth's orbit, during the separation of one of the spacecraft's modules, an unexpected accident occurred. An oxygen tank exploded, causing a catastrophic loss of power and air. Suddenly, the mission to the moon wasn't the goal anymore. The new goal was survival.

What makes the Apollo 13 story so incredible is how everyone adapted. The astronauts and the team on the ground rethought their tools, their timelines, and their strategies.

They used whatever was available—including duct tape and plastic bags—to solve problems like cleaning carbon dioxide from the air.

In the end, the Apollo 13 mission didn't achieve its original goal, but it was still a success. The astronauts came home alive, proving that clear goals, the right tools, and adaptability can turn chaos into triumph.

MY OWN ENCOUNTER WITH ENTROPY

When I first started my business in 1988, I thought, How hard can it be? I didn't know anything about business, economics, or entropy, but I knew how to work and never give up. Growing up poor on a farm taught me things go sideways, usually at the worst possible time. The cows need to be milked twice a day, no matter what's gone wrong or whether you're sick. Not milking is not an option.

Farm life also made me good at solving problems on the fly. You get the tractor stuck; you get it out. You have a leaky water bowl; you fix it with the tools and spare parts you have on hand. And if you've ever driven by a farm and wondered why there's old equipment lying around, that's not laziness—that's practicality. Those machines are a treasure trove of spare parts when the cows need milking, and the nearest supplier is a hundred miles away.

This upbringing gave me the confidence to deal with surprises and keep going no matter what. But I didn't understand interest rate fluctuations, geopolitical upheavals like the Gulf Wars, or major crises like 9/11.

Every time I scraped through by the skin of my teeth, some new calamity would crop up. It was exhausting. Eventually, I realized the problem wasn't the chaos—it was my expectation that stability and comfort were normal.

They're not. Chaos is the norm. Once I accepted that, I stopped waiting for things to 'settle down,' and started adapting to the storm instead of fighting it.

RESPECTING ENTROPY (AND CHOOSING YOUR BATTLES)

If you're wondering how to fight entropy, here's the secret: you can't. You can slow it down, mitigate its effects, and prepare for its inevitable chaos, but you'll never beat it.

The best thing you can do is respect its power and focus your energy on what you can control. For example, don't waste time obsessing over keeping your car spotless.

Entropy is going to win that battle. Instead, spend your time and resources on things that actually matter—like maintaining the engine so it runs, or making sure your loved ones are buckled in safely.

You can't control the rust, but you can control what's important.

HUMILITY IN THE FACE OF LUCK

Let's be honest—when things go well, it's tempting to take all the credit.

But here's the reality: even your biggest successes likely involved some amount of luck.

Recognizing this doesn't diminish your hard work—it just keeps you humble and helps you make smarter choices moving forward.

Think of it this way: If you attribute all your success to skill and none to luck, you might get overconfident and start taking bigger, riskier bets.

That's when entropy and chaos will remind you who's boss. Stay humble, and you'll avoid falling into that trap.

CLOSING THOUGHT

Entropy and chaos are constants, but luck is unpredictable.

The best you can do is respect all three. Prepare for the challenges you can see, adapt when life throws you a curveball, and be grateful when luck works in your favor.

Because in the game of life, it's not about eliminating chaos—it's about learning to live with it.

CHAPTER TWO

The Value of Time and Energy

What's more valuable: time, energy, or money?

If your first thought was money, I've got news for you—you're already playing the game with the wrong rules. While money is important, it's also replenishable. You can lose money and make it back. But time? Once it's gone, it's gone.

And energy? That tank empties faster and faster as you age.

This chapter is about understanding these finite resources and using them wisely.

THE FINITE NATURE OF TIME

Time is the great equalizer. Whether you're a billionaire or struggling to make ends meet, you get 24 hours in a day. What separates those who succeed from those who stay stuck isn't how much time they have—it's how they use it.

Let's break it down:

- **Time is non-refundable:** You can't get back the minutes you spent doom-scrolling or watching TV.
- **Time can be exchanged**: You can trade time for money (working a job) or trade money for time (hiring someone to do a task). The key is knowing when each trade makes sense.

- **Time is opportunity:** Every moment spent on one thing is a moment you can't spend on something else. Are you spending your time on what truly matters?

THE ENERGY EQUATION

If time is the clock, energy is the fuel.

You wake up every morning with a limited amount of energy to spend, and how you use it determines how far you'll get.

But here's the catch: energy declines over time.

What you could power through at 25, might feel impossible at 55.

The lesson? Spend your energy where it counts.

Don't waste it on trivial things that don't bring you closer to your goals.

And remember, rest isn't laziness—it's refueling for what matters most.

THE COST-BENEFIT LENS

To make the most of your time and energy, you need to evaluate every decision through a cost-benefit lens. Let me share a story that illustrates this perfectly.

When I was about 15, my sister-in-law asked if I wanted an orange. Now, I like oranges well enough, but I hesitated. Peeling an orange?

That's effort. I politely declined. But then she said, "What if I peel it for you?" Suddenly, the cost (my effort) was gone, and the benefit (enjoying the orange) outweighed it.

I happily accepted.

It sounds silly, but that moment stuck with me. To this day, I subconsciously weigh every decision: Is the cost worth the benefit? If not, why bother?

THE INTERNET: THE NEW BILLBOARDS

Every time you scroll through your favorite app or browse the web, you're bombarded with links begging for your attention. Some are entertaining, some are educational, and some are designed to make your blood boil.

But here's the question you should always ask: Does clicking this link benefit me, or does it benefit someone else?

The truth is, that every click generates money for someone. It doesn't really matter who. Advertisers, website owners, content creators—someone, somewhere, is profiting from your attention.

And in many cases, they're not just profiting—they're actively using tools like outrage to grab your eyeballs.

OUTRAGE: THE ULTIMATE ATTENTION MAGNET

Outrage is one of the most powerful tools in the Money Game. Why? Because it works. Nothing gets people clicking and commenting faster than a headline designed to rile them up.

Every time you click on an outrageous article, watch a sensationalized video or argue in the comments section, you're making someone else money. You're spending your time and energy playing into their hands.

Here's the hard truth: it doesn't matter if the content makes you angry, entertained, or confused. What matters is that you've given it your attention, and that attention is worth money.

More eyeballs mean more revenue, and outrage is one of the cheapest, easiest ways to get those eyeballs.

DON'T BE PLAYED

The next time you're about to click on a link, stop and ask yourself:

- Who benefits from this click?
- Is this content adding value to my life, or am I just fueling someone else's profit machine?

- Am I spending my time and energy wisely, or am I falling into the outrage trap?

Remember, time and energy are finite resources. Once spent, you can't get them back.

Don't waste them on content that does nothing for you except distract, frustrate, or manipulate.

TIME, ENERGY, AND MONEY: A BALANCING ACT

Here's where things get tricky. Time, energy, and money are interconnected, and the balance among them is different for everyone.

- If you have more money, you can buy back time and save energy by outsourcing tasks.
- If you have more time, you can save money by doing things yourself.
- If you have energy to spare, you can invest it in building something that pays off in the long run.

The key is to evaluate your situation and make choices that align with your goals. For example:

- Should you spend an hour mowing the lawn or pay someone to do it so you can work on your side hustle?
- Should you cook at home to save money or order takeout to save time?

There's no right answer—it depends on what's most valuable to you at that moment.

INVESTING YOUR RESOURCES WISELY

Think of time, energy, and money as investments. Before you spend them, ask yourself:

- **What's the return?** Does this action align with my goals and move me closer to achieving them?
- **Is it worth it?** Are the benefits greater than the costs?

- **Am I being honest with myself?** Sometimes we convince ourselves something is necessary when it's not.

A wise investment of your resources brings you closer to the life you want. A poor investment leaves you drained and further from your goals.

CLOSING THOUGHT

Time and energy are finite.

Money is important, but it's replenishable—time and energy are not. The most successful people aren't the ones who have the most money; they're the ones who use their time and energy wisely.

So the next time you're faced with a decision, ask yourself: Is this a good investment of my resources?

If not, it might be time to peel back the layers and focus on what really matters.

CHAPTER THREE

Start at the End: Building Your Road Map

f you don't know where you're going, how will you know when you've arrived?

It's a simple question, but it's one most people never ask themselves. They drift through life, reacting to whatever comes their way, instead of planning for what they truly want.

If you want to succeed—whether it's in finances, relationships, or personal growth—you need to start at the end.

Define your ultimate goal, and then work backward to create a road map for how to get there.

WHY START AT THE END?

Starting at the end gives you clarity. It compels you to reflect on your true desires and the reasons behind them.

Without a clear destination, you'll waste time and energy chasing the wrong things or getting distracted by opportunities that don't align with your values.

Imagine planning a road trip without deciding on a destination. You might end up driving in circles, wasting gas, and feeling frustrated.

But if you know where you're going, you can map out the most efficient route and enjoy the journey.

ASK THE RIGHT QUESTIONS

To start at the end, you need to ask yourself some important questions:

1) **What is my dream?** Be specific. What do you want to achieve, and why does it matter to you?

2) **When do I want to achieve it?** Set a timeline. Goals without deadlines are just wishes.

3) **How much time do I have?** Be realistic about your age, health, and other factors that might affect your timeline.

4) **What obstacles will I face?** Acknowledge the headwinds of entropy and chaos that will inevitably arise.

5) **What resources do I have?** Take stock of your time, energy, money, skills, and support network.

6) **What are my strengths?** What are your natural strengths, and what activities bring you joy?

7) **What are my weaknesses?** What tasks or areas do you struggle with, or would you rather avoid?

8) **What do I like doing, and what would I rather not do?** Focus your assets on doing what you enjoy and excel at. Delegate weak areas to people who like doing those tasks and are skilled in areas where you are not.

By aligning your efforts with your strengths and passions, and delegating where needed, you'll not only achieve more but also enjoy the process.

Building a support system of people who complement your skills is a powerful strategy for long-term success.

REVERSE ENGINEERING SUCCESS

Once you've defined your goal, the next step is to work backward. What key steps must be accomplished along the journey?

What actions do you need to take today, this month, or this year to move closer to your destination?

Let's take an example:

Your goal is to achieve early retirement and explore the world. That's great—but what does it actually mean? How much money will you need to retire comfortably?

How will you save that money? Will you need to downsize your lifestyle, invest in rental properties, or start a side hustle?

By breaking the goal into smaller, actionable steps, you make it manageable and achievable.

THE IMPORTANCE OF FLEXIBILITY

Even the best-laid plans will need to adapt to changing circumstances.

Life is unpredictable, and your road map might need to be adjusted along the way. Maybe a new opportunity arises that accelerates your timeline, or maybe a setback forces you to recalibrate.

That's okay. Flexibility doesn't mean abandoning your goal—it means finding a better route when the road ahead is blocked. And sometimes there isn't a better route, but there are always alternate routes. Then, you have to pick the least painful detour.

But don't confuse flexibility with indecision. There's a difference between adjusting your plan and constantly changing your mind. Stay focused on the end goal, and let it guide your decisions.

THE POWER OF VISUALIZATION

Starting at the end isn't just about planning—it's about belief. Visualizing your success can be incredibly motivating. Picture yourself achieving your goal. What does it feel like? What does it look like? The clearer you can visualize it, the more tangible it feels—and the more motivated you'll be to take the steps required to bring it to life.

Here's a tip: Write down your goal and keep it somewhere visible. Maybe it's a sticky note on your mirror or a screensaver on your phone. Seeing your goal every day reminds you of what you're working toward and keeps you focused.

If you are able to put your goal into a visual, it will multiply your resolve. A photograph of a beach, a classic car, your family smiling, whatever it is, if you can not only visualize it but SEE it... its power multiplies in your brain.

SMALL STEPS, BIG RESULTS

Here's the good news: You don't have to achieve your goal overnight. Success is the result of consistent, incremental progress. Every small step you take—whether it's saving a little more money, learning a new skill, or saying no to distractions—brings you closer to the life you want.

Let me give you an example from my own life. When I was 16, I set a goal to buy a house and start my own business. I didn't know all the steps it would take, but I knew what the end looked like.

I started small—working long hours, saving every penny, and learning from every mistake. I reached my goal by the time I turned 22. It wasn't easy, but knowing exactly what I was working toward kept me motivated.

THE DREAM VS. NIGHTMARE TEST

Finally, remember your goal isn't just about achieving a dream—it's about avoiding a nightmare.

What's the worst-case scenario if you don't achieve your goal?

Use that as fuel to keep pushing forward. Whether it's the fear of financial instability, the regret of wasted potential, or the loss of freedom, let your nightmare remind you why your goal is worth fighting for.

CLOSING THOUGHT

Starting at the end isn't just a strategy—it's a mindset.

It's about taking control of your life, defining your destination, and creating a road map to get there.

So take a moment to ask yourself: Where do I want to go? What does success look like to me? And what steps can I take today to start moving in that direction?

The journey won't always be easy, but with a clear destination in mind, every step will bring you closer to the life you've always wanted.

CHAPTER FOUR

The True Value of Money

oney. It's one of the most powerful tools in the world—and one of the most misunderstood. People spend their entire lives chasing it, hoarding it, and worrying about it.

But here's the truth: money isn't an end in itself. It's a tool. It's not what brings happiness, success, or fulfillment. What matters is how you use it and what you trade for it.

Making Money is Hard... at First. Spending Money is Easy.

Here's the first problem with money: It's hard to earn, especially in the beginning when you're starting from scratch.

Whether you're working long hours at your first job, building a business, or trying to climb the career ladder, making money requires time, effort, and persistence.

But as you gain experience, build skills, and grow your resources, it gets easier—if you play the game right.

Now here's the kicker: While making money can be hard, spending it is ridiculously easy. Everywhere you look, someone is trying to separate you from your money.

Advertisements tell you what you 'need,' social pressures encourage you to keep up with others, and convenience tempts you to choose the easy (and often expensive) option.

Every dollar you spend is a step backward—unless it's spent on something that increases your likelihood of getting closer to your goal.

Practice assessing every spending decision with this question: Does this increase or decrease my chances of achieving my goal?

THE COFFEE MAKER EXPERIMENT

Now let's take this a step further. Imagine you buy a $30 coffee maker and make your coffee at home every morning for just $1.

By doing this, you save $6 a day compared to buying coffee from a café. What happens if you invest that $6 daily savings at a 6% annual return?

Here's the math:

- Over five years, your daily savings of $6 would grow to approximately **$13,046**, even after accounting for the initial $30 spent on the coffee maker.
- At that point, the $13,046 investment would generate **$780 per year** in passive income at a 6% annual return.

But what happens if you keep saving and investing for 10 years instead of five? Let's run the numbers:

- After 10 years, your daily $6 savings would grow to approximately **$30,544**, thanks to consistent saving and the power of compounding at a 6% annual return.
- That $30,544 investment would generate **$1,827 per year**, or approximately **$152.72 per month**, in passive income.

With small, consistent changes like redirecting your coffee budget into investments, you're not just saving money—you're creating a long-term income stream that works for you.

THE $70,000 TRUCK QUESTION

How many people do you know who are driving a $70,000 car or pickup truck while living in a mobile home? Let's break this down.

Borrowing $70,000 to buy a truck at a 6% annual interest rate and paying it off over seven years results in a monthly loan payment of approximately **$1,022.60**. Add to that the ongoing costs:

- Fuel: **$200/month**
- Maintenance: **$250/month**
- Insurance: **$150/month**

That brings the total monthly cost of owning the vehicle to approximately **$1,622.60**.

Over seven years, that adds up to over **$136,700** spent on a depreciating asset.

And here's the kicker: after seven years, the $70,000 truck has likely lost most of its value.

Vehicles, especially expensive ones, typically depreciate rapidly, leaving you with a financial loss on top of the ongoing costs.

THE SMARTER ALTERNATIVE

Now, let's explore a smarter alternative. Instead of buying a $70,000 truck, you purchase a reliable, inexpensive vehicle for **$10,000**.

If you really need a truck for work, just buy an inexpensive and reliable used truck. This reduces your monthly costs significantly:

- Loan payment (5 years at 6% interest): **$193.33/month**
- Fuel: **$150/month**
- Maintenance: **$250/month**
- Insurance: **$100/month**

This brings the total monthly cost of owning the inexpensive vehicle to approximately **$693.33**—a savings of **$929.27/month** compared to the

$70,000 truck. Over five years, this savings amounts to approximately **$55,756.25**.

Now, instead of putting $70,000 into a truck, you take **$50,000** and invest it in a piece of real estate with an 8% annual appreciation. After seven years, that real estate investment grows to approximately **$85,691**. This creates a vastly different financial outcome:

The real estate appreciates significantly, generating wealth over time.

The inexpensive vehicle provides reliable transportation while keeping monthly costs low.

After seven years, you own a tangible asset worth over **$85,000**, compared to a depreciated vehicle that is likely worth little to nothing.

THE PEOPLE WITH WHOM YOU ASSOCIATE

Now, let's take a step back. What influences your decisions about buying a truck versus saving and investing? It's often the people we associate with—their values, priorities, and what they consider 'normal.'

This influence is particularly strong when it comes to romantic partners or potential partners. Are you trying to impress someone with a shiny new truck? Or do you share a vision of financial independence and long-term growth?

Here's a gentle reminder: The people around us, whether friends, family or a significant other, have an extraordinary impact on how we view money. Choosing to spend $1,500 a month on a truck might feel perfectly reasonable if everyone in your circle is doing the same.

But if you're surrounded by people who prioritize saving and investing, you'll likely start to see the $70,000 truck in a different light.

We will dive deeper into this idea in the chapter about like-minded people. For now, remember that who you surround yourself with can significantly influence your financial success—or your financial struggles.

And yes, this includes the romantic partner who might not be impressed by your growing investment portfolio but loves the roar of your truck's engine.

(*Hint:* maybe it's time to have a chat about shared goals! Or, maybe, install a button on your used sedan that makes the noise of a big truck, for his/her benefit!)

THE TAKEAWAY

This example isn't about criticizing anyone's choices—it's about understanding the long-term impact of those choices.

Ask yourself: Is buying this truck taking me closer to or further away from my goal of financial freedom? Every decision matters in the Money Game, and understanding the true cost of your spending habits is critical to winning that game.

This is a very important rule in the Money Game:

If you're spending money that was not generated by a return on an investment, you're losing the game.

Some cultures teach their children from a very young age never to spend money until it's grown tenfold.

If you need something that costs $10, the expectation is to grow that initial $10 investment into $100 before spending it.

This mindset reinforces discipline, patience, and a long-term perspective on wealth creation—key attributes for winning the Money Game.

CHAPTER FIVE

The Rules of the Money Game

ife is full of games.

Some are literal, like soccer or chess, where the rules are written and obvious.

Others, like the Money Game, are subtle—hidden in plain sight. In capitalism, the rules aren't just about economics; they shape the very fabric of society.

And if you don't understand them, the game will play you.

RULE 1: KNOW THE RULES BEFORE YOU PLAY

Imagine sitting down to a game of chess, but you've never seen a chessboard before. You'd have no idea what the pieces do, what the objective is, or even where to start.

That's how most people approach money; they jump in without ever learning the rules. In capitalism, one of the rules is efficiency. The system is designed to reward those who understand how to work within it.

That means hard work, yes, but also education—formal or informal—and a willingness to take calculated risks.

But here's the catch: most people don't realize they're playing a game, let alone there are rules. They're busy earning and spending, never stopping to ask, Am I playing this game well?

RULE 2: MONEY IS A TOOL, NOT THE GOAL

Money isn't happiness. It isn't a success. It is a means to an end.

Yet so many people treat money as the end goal, chasing it blindly without asking themselves, What am I really trying to achieve?

The rule here is simple: Use money to create opportunities, security, and freedom. Spend it intentionally on things that truly matter to you.

Invest it wisely so it can work for you. Money sitting idle or spent on frivolous things doesn't grow.

But money invested strategically can generate returns that give you more freedom and security.

RULE 3: PLAY OFFENSE AND DEFENSE

Most people are good at one side of the game—either making money (offense) or saving and protecting money (defense).

The winners? They master both. Offense is about earning more, finding opportunities, and increasing your income streams.

Defense is about keeping what you earn, avoiding unnecessary expenses, and investing wisely.

For example, it's great to focus on increasing your income, but if you're spending it as fast as you make it—or faster—you're not making progress.

Similarly, being frugal isn't enough if you're not actively growing your wealth. Balance both sides of the equation, and you'll be unstoppable.

RULE 4: DON'T LET THE SYSTEM PLAY YOU

Capitalism is efficient, but it's also ruthless. Advertisements, social pressures, and marketing campaigns are designed to separate you from your money.

Every billboard, commercial, and internet link you click on is part of a game someone else is playing to make money from you.

Ask yourself: Does this benefit me, or does it benefit them? If it's not helping you get closer to your financial goals, you're likely being played.

This is especially true when it comes to debt. Credit card companies and lenders thrive on people who don't understand the true cost of borrowing.

Every dollar of interest you pay is a dollar lost to someone else's game.

RULE 5: INVEST BEFORE YOU SPEND

This rule is straightforward but crucial: If you're spending money that wasn't generated by a return on an investment, you're losing the game.

Some cultures teach their children to grow their money tenfold before spending it.

The idea is simple: Let your money work for you first. Then, and only then, should you consider spending it.

For example, if you want to buy a $6 coffee, calculate how much you'd need to invest to generate that $6 daily.

Only when your investments are covering your expenses are you truly free.

RULE 6: TIME, ENERGY, AND MONEY ARE INTERCHANGEABLE

Time and energy are finite.

You can trade them for money, but you can also trade money to save time and energy.

The key is understanding the value of each resource in your life and using them strategically.

Think about it:

Is it worth spending an hour clipping coupons to save $5 if your time is worth $50 an hour? Probably not.

But investing a few hours learning a new skill that could increase your earning potential?

That's a worthwhile trade.

THE CAPITALIST PARADOX

Here's the irony: Capitalism is designed to reward financial literacy, yet many people in capitalist societies lack it.

They're taught through marketing and societal pressures that spending money will make them happy.

This couldn't be further from the truth.

The real path to financial freedom lies in understanding the rules and playing the game to your advantage.

Save money, invest it wisely, and let your returns cover your expenses. That's how you win.

THE TAKEAWAY

The Money Game is unwinnable if you don't know the rules. But once you understand them, the system becomes your ally, not your adversary. Remember:

- Learn the rules before you play.
- Use money as a tool, not a goal.
- Balance offense and defense.
- Don't let the system play you.
- Invest before you spend.
- Value your time, energy, and money.

The rules are simple, but following them requires discipline and awareness. Once you master these principles, you'll find yourself not just surviving, but thriving in the Money Game.

CHAPTER SIX

Time, Energy, and Money—Your Three Most Valuable Resources

When it comes to winning the Money Game, most people think it's all about the money.

But the truth is, money is just one of the three key resources you have at your disposal. The other two—time and energy—are far more finite and precious. You can always make more money, but you can't create more time, and your energy decreases with age.

If you want to succeed financially, and in life, you need to learn how to manage all three resources strategically. This chapter will show you how.

THE MYTH OF INFINITE TIME

Let's get one thing straight: Time is your most valuable resource. Why? Because it's non-renewable.

Once it's gone, it's gone forever. And yet, people waste time as though they have an endless supply.

Imagine this: You're given $86,400 every morning, but at the end of the day, whatever you haven't spent disappears. Would you let even a single dollar go to waste?

Of course not. But here's the kicker: You're already living that reality. You get 86,400 seconds every day, and whatever you don't use is gone forever.

The key question is, Are you spending your time wisely, or are you letting it slip through your fingers?

ENERGY: THE INVISIBLE CURRENCY

Energy is like the fuel in your tank. It powers everything you do, from your job to your relationships to your hobbies. But unlike time, energy doesn't stay constant—it fluctuates daily, and it declines as you age.

When you wake up in the morning, you have a finite amount of energy. Every decision you make, every task you complete, and every stressful situation you encounter, depletes it. This is why it's critical to focus your energy on things that truly matter.

The rule here is simple: Invest your energy where it will give you the greatest return.

That means working on tasks that align with your goals, nurturing meaningful relationships, and avoiding unnecessary distractions.

MONEY: THE FLEXIBLE RESOURCE

While time and energy are finite, money is different. It's renewable, flexible, and—when managed correctly—it can even buy you more time and energy.

Here's the thing, though: Most people misuse money. They trade their finite time and energy for it, then squander it on things that don't align with their goals. The key to winning the Money Game is to reverse this equation: Use money to save time and conserve energy.

For example:

- Hiring someone to mow your lawn frees up hours you can spend on more valuable pursuits.

- Automating bill payments reduces mental clutter, allowing you to focus on higher-priority tasks.

The question to ask yourself is: Am I using money to improve my life, or am I letting it control me?

A PERSONAL ANECDOTE: THE PEPPER GRINDER

When I was about 15, my brother helped me get a job at a butcher supply company. They sold all kinds of things—spices, sausage casings, food additives—but my job was running the pepper-grinding machine. Sounds simple, right? Let me tell you, it wasn't.

The process started with dumping 50-pound bags of whole black or white peppercorns into the hopper. The machine would then grind them into fine pepper powder. Black pepper was bad enough, but grinding white pepper was downright brutal.

The fine powder filled the air, and no matter how much I tried to avoid it, I'd end up coughing so hard I'd throw up. My clothes would reek of pepper, and it clung to my skin like a second layer.

If that wasn't bad enough, there was another key lesson: wash your hands **before and after** going to the bathroom. Let's just say pepper dust and certain sensitive areas of the body don't mix.

It's a mistake you make only once. By the end of my shifts, my sinuses felt like they were on fire. To this day, I don't think they've fully recovered. I don't use much spice in my food, and I can barely smell anything.

The cost of that experience? My time, my energy, and a little bit of my physical well-being. The payoff? Not much—minimum wage for a brutal day's work and some valuable life lessons.

THE LESSONS LEARNED

That job taught me a few things about time, energy, and money that I still carry with me today:

1) **Time**: Time is finite. If you're going to trade it for money, make sure it's worth it. Are you building skills? Gaining experience? Or just grinding away with no future benefit?

2) **Energy**: Your energy is precious. If you burn through it on things that don't align with your goals, you'll have nothing left for the things that do. Grinding pepper was a waste of energy—physically taxing with no long-term reward.

3) **Health**: No amount of money is worth sacrificing your health. The pepper job taught me to think critically about the long-term costs of short-term gains.

THE MULTIPLIER EFFECT

Here's where it all comes together. When you use money wisely, it saves you time and energy.

When you invest your time and energy effectively, it generates more money. This creates a virtuous cycle—a multiplier effect—that propels you closer to your goals.

For example:

- Investing time in learning a new skill increases your earning potential (money).
- Using money to delegate mundane tasks frees up time for higher-value activities.
- Conserving energy by focusing on meaningful work improves your productivity, leading to greater financial success.

THE TAKEAWAY

The pepper grinder job is a reminder that not all work is created equal. Some jobs teach you skills or open doors to new opportunities.

Others teach you what not to do with your time and energy. The key is to evaluate every decision through the lens of cost and benefit—time, energy, and money. If the costs outweigh the benefits, it's time to rethink your approach.

Time, energy, and money are your three most valuable resources. Mastering how to use them wisely is the key to winning the Money Game—and life.

Remember:

- Time is finite; don't waste it.
- Energy is precious; invest it where it counts.
- Money is renewable; use it to create opportunities, not liabilities.

Every decision you make affects this balance. The better you manage these resources, the closer you'll get to achieving your goals—and the happier and freer you will become.

CHAPTER SEVEN

The People With Whom You Associate

WHY YOUR CIRCLE MATTERS

There's an old saying: *"You're the average of the five people you spend the most time with"* - Jim Rohn. While that might not be scientifically precise, the sentiment is spot on. The people you surround yourself with influence how you think, act, and—most importantly in the Money Game—how you spend.

If your circle values flashy cars, expensive dinners, and living beyond their means, chances are you'll find yourself trying to keep up. On the other hand, if you surround yourself with people who prioritize saving, investing, and learning, you'll naturally adopt those habits too.

The question is: Are the people in your life helping you move closer to your financial goals—or further away?

ROMANTIC PARTNERS: A MAKE-OR-BREAK FACTOR

When it comes to financial success, few relationships have as much impact as your romantic partner.

Your partner's financial habits, priorities, and values will shape your own decisions in profound ways.

Let's face it:

Financial disagreements are one of the leading causes of stress in relationships.

If one partner is a spender and the other is a saver, it's like having one foot on the gas and the other on the brake.

The result? Frustration and burnout.

The key is alignment. That doesn't mean you have to agree on every detail, but you should share the same overall goals and priorities.

Do you both value financial freedom?

Are you both willing to make sacrifices to get there?

These are the questions that determine whether you're a winning team—or setting yourselves up for failure.

One way to check if you're aligned is to think about how you handle goals and routines together.

Shared habits—like discussing finances regularly or planning together—can make a significant difference in staying on track.

A PERSONAL ANECDOTE: THE TRUCK DEBATE

Let me give you a personal example. My wife and I are both horse enthusiasts, and we travel quite a bit with our horses. As you can imagine, this involves owning trucks and trailers, which are expensive to maintain.

Now, I'm the type who sees these vehicles as tools—practical, functional, and not worth stressing over. My truck has a few dings and scratches because, frankly, I don't care as long as it runs.

My wife, on the other hand, keeps her truck in pristine condition. She doesn't understand how I can be so casual about something so expensive, and I don't understand why she spends so much energy keeping hers perfect.

But here's the thing: We both respect each other's perspective, and we make sure our decisions align with our shared financial goals.

One of the ways we stay on the same page is through a routine we both value deeply. Most mornings, we spend an hour in bed together, enjoying coffee, playing Wordle, and discussing our plans for the day.

This isn't just downtime—it's a chance to revisit our long-term goals, reflect on our progress, and ensure we're still heading in the right direction.

It's one of the ways we stay connected and aligned, both in life and in our financial priorities. When you think about shared goals, it's a lot like driving a team of horses.

If the horses are pulling in the same direction, you'll make steady progress toward your destination. But if they're pulling in opposite directions? You'll just go in circles, or worse, get stuck in place. In relationships—especially when it comes to finances—it's critical to make sure the horses are pulling together. If not, ask yourself:

Are we getting closer to our goals, or are we just spinning our wheels?

The lesson? Even when you have different priorities, shared values and routines can keep you on track.

When you're both committed to the same long-term vision, those differences become less about friction and more about balance.

THE SOCIAL PRESSURE TRAP

Have you ever noticed how some people buy expensive cars, clothes, or gadgets, not because they need them, but because they want to impress others? This is the social pressure trap at work. It's not just about keeping up with the Joneses—it's about competing with them.

But here's the thing: The Joneses probably aren't winning the Money Game either. They're likely drowning in debt, living paycheck to paycheck, and putting on a facade of success. Why would you want to emulate that?

The solution? Surround yourself with people who value substance over appearance. Find friends who understand the importance of financial stability and who won't judge you for driving a practical car or skipping that overpriced dinner.

THE INFLUENCE OF SHARED VALUES

It's not just about avoiding bad influences—it's about actively seeking out good ones.

When you spend time with people who are disciplined, goal-oriented, and financially savvy, their habits will rub off on you.

Think of it like osmosis: Surround yourself with the *right* people, and you'll absorb their mindset and values without even realizing it.

You will find yourself making better financial decisions simply because it's the norm in your circle.

PRACTICAL TIPS FOR BUILDING YOUR CIRCLE

- **Audit Your Current Circle**: Take a close look at the people you spend the most time with. Are they helping or hindering your progress?
- **Seek Out Like-Minded Individuals**: Join communities, attend workshops, or participate in online groups where financial literacy and personal growth are valued.
- **Have Honest Conversations**: Talk to your friends and family about your goals. You might be surprised how supportive they can be—or how resistant they are to change. Either way, you'll gain clarity.
- **Prioritize Quality Over Quantity**: It's better to have a few supportive, like-minded friends than a large group who drain your time, energy, and money.

THE TAKEAWAY

The people in your life matter more than you think. They influence how you think, act, and spend. Surround yourself with people who share your values and goals, and you'll naturally gravitate toward success.

Remember:

- Your circle should align with your financial priorities.
- Social pressure is a trap—avoid it.
- Shared values in relationships are non-negotiable.

In the Money Game, your team can make or break your success. Choose wisely.

CHAPTER EIGHT

The Power of Ownership

WHY OWNERSHIP MATTERS

Ownership is one of the most critical concepts in the Money Game, yet it's often misunderstood. At its core, ownership isn't just about having things—it's about control, responsibility, and the ability to build wealth and freedom over time. Ownership can take many forms, from owning a home to running a business, holding investments, or even owning your decisions and goals.

On the flip side, blaming others for your woes is an excellent way of not being successful. When you point fingers at external forces—whether it's the government, your upbringing, or the competition—you're giving away control. And when you hang out with people who make a habit of blaming others for their problems, you're surrounding yourself with negativity and excuses instead of solutions and progress.

THE SQUIRREL ANALOGY

Have you ever watched a squirrel gather nuts as it prepares for winter? Does it sit around with other unhappy squirrels, complaining about how tough they have it?

Does it blame the 'squirrel government' for the lack of acorns or rant about the neighboring squirrels stealing their stash?

Of course not. The squirrel works hard every day gathering nuts because winter is coming, and if it doesn't, it—and its family—might not survive.

The squirrel doesn't waste time wishing it were born a lion or a whale, nor does it lament the unfairness of being small and vulnerable.

It simply accepts the hand it's been dealt as part of nature's great game and does the best it can.

Now, imagine what would happen if the squirrel didn't try. What if it spent its days complaining instead of working?

What if it taught its young to blame the squirrel government for their struggles or resent other squirrels who came from different territories in search of nuts?

It doesn't take much imagination to see how quickly that family of squirrels would perish.

The lesson is clear: Complaining doesn't solve problems. Taking responsibility does. The squirrel's approach to life isn't just instinct—it's a powerful reminder of the rules of the game:

Work hard, take care of yourself and your family, and focus on what you can control.

THE GOVERNMENT IS NOT GOING TO TAKE CARE OF YOU

One of the most important rules in the Money Game is this: The government is not going to take care of you.

In fact, the government is one of the things trying to separate you from your money.

This isn't to say the government is inherently bad or that politicians are evil. It's simply to recognize the reality of the system.

Politicians, regardless of their party or country, are looking out for their own interests—namely, staying in power.

Their decisions, policies, and promises are designed to further their political careers, not necessarily your personal well-being.

So, the next time a government program, tax cut, or new policy is introduced, ask yourself:

Is this truly good for me and my family, or is it good for the politician or party selling it to me?

The answer is often the latter.

This is why it's so important to take ownership of your financial future. Relying on the government—or anyone else—to solve your problems is a losing strategy.

The Money Game is yours to play, and the sooner you accept that responsibility, the sooner you can start winning.

TAKING RESPONSIBILITY

Taking responsibility means owning your actions, your decisions, and your future. It's about saying, "This is my life, and I'm in charge of it."

Blaming others might feel good in the moment, but it doesn't solve anything. Worse, it trains your mind to look for excuses instead of opportunities.

Surrounding yourself with people who blame others is equally dangerous. These are the people who will pull you down, distract you from your goals, and convince you success is out of reach.

If you want to win the Money Game, you need to align yourself with people who understand the rules—people who take responsibility for their own lives and encourage you to do the same.

WHAT OWNERSHIP REALLY MEANS

Ownership isn't just about possessions—it's about control. When you own something, you have the power to decide how it's used, managed, or leveraged.

This applies not only to physical assets like houses and cars, but also to intangible assets like your time, skills, and ideas.

The opposite of ownership is **dependency**. When you rent an apartment, work for someone else, or rely on credit to make ends meet, you're dependent on others for your stability and success.

While dependency isn't always bad, the more you own, the more control you have over your life.

THE LONG-TERM BENEFITS OF OWNERSHIP

Ownership creates stability, control, and the potential for growth. When you own something—whether it's a house, a business, or a portfolio of investments—you're building a foundation for the future.

Over time, the value of what you own can grow, generating passive income and creating opportunities you might not have otherwise.

Ownership isn't always easy. It requires sacrifice, responsibility, and a willingness to take risks. But the rewards—financial freedom, independence, and the ability to live life on your terms—are worth it.

THE TAKEAWAY

Ownership is the cornerstone of financial success. It's about more than having things—it's about taking control of your life, building wealth, and creating freedom. To win the Money Game, focus on:

- Acquiring assets that generate income and grow in value.
- Minimizing liabilities that drain your resources.
- Taking responsibility for your decisions and actions.

- Avoiding the trap of blaming others—and avoiding people who do.

- Recognizing the government isn't your savior—it's part of the system you need to navigate.

The question isn't just, What do I own? It's;

"What do I control?" Because in the end, control is the true measure of ownership—and the key to winning the Money Game.

CHAPTER NINE

The Role of Education and Continuous Learning

WHY EDUCATION MATTERS

Education isn't just about degrees, diplomas, or certifications. It's about developing the ability to think critically, solve problems, and adapt to a constantly changing world. In the Money Game, those who understand the rules—and how to adapt to new ones—are the ones who thrive.

One of the most dangerous things you can believe is that you already know enough. The truth is, the more you learn, the more you realize how much you don't know. This humility is the cornerstone of continuous learning.

THE REAL COST OF IGNORANCE

It's often said that "ignorance is bliss," but in the Money Game, ignorance is expensive. Think about it:

- If you don't understand how credit card interest works, you could end up paying thousands in unnecessary fees.
- If you don't educate yourself about investing, you might miss out on the compounding growth that could secure your retirement.

- If you don't learn how to budget, you might find yourself continually battling to stay financially afloat.

In a world filled with marketing traps, misinformation, and financial pitfalls, not knowing the rules is like walking blindfolded through a minefield.

A NEW PERSPECTIVE: MY FIRST TRIP TO MEXICO

In 1998, I was fortunate enough to be recommended to a Mexican company for our products and services.

This was a potential game-changer for my business, and I jumped at the opportunity.

Before that, I had never been to Mexico and had no idea what to expect.

The plant I visited turned out to be one of the most advanced facilities I had ever seen—not just compared to plants in Mexico, but to those in Canada and the USA as well.

The owners, who were highly educated in the USA, gave me a detailed tour of the facility and shared their vision for the future. Their passion, intelligence, and innovation were inspiring.

On the plane ride home, I had a moment of clarity: I needed to learn Spanish. If I wanted to build strong relationships and continue working in Mexico, understanding the language was non-negotiable.

Upon my return, I immediately enrolled in Spanish classes.

Little did I know how critical that decision would be.

WHEN 9/11 HIT: WAS IT LUCK?

Fast forward to September 11, 2001. Like everyone else, I watched in shock and disbelief as the tragedy unfolded.

But the effects weren't just emotional—they were deeply personal and immediate. The U.S. border with Canada closed, and for months, I couldn't get anything into or out of the USA.

At the time, most of our business was in the U.S. I was hanging by a thread business-wise, and bankruptcy felt like a very real possibility.

But here's the twist: it was the Latin American sales, particularly in Mexico, that saved us.

Those relationships I had worked hard to build, the language I had committed to learning, and the trust we had developed with our partners in Mexico were what kept us afloat during one of the most challenging times in my business career. So, was it luck? Maybe. But it wasn't just luck. It was a preparation meeting opportunity.

I had made the decision years earlier to expand into Latin America and invest in understanding the culture and language.

That foresight, combined with the strength of those relationships, made all the difference.

The lesson? You can't predict every crisis, but you can prepare yourself to weather them.

Education, adaptability, and building strong connections are the tools that turn potential disasters into survivable setbacks—and sometimes even opportunities.

THE ROLE OF CONTINUOUS LEARNING

Whether it's learning a new language, understanding a market, or developing a skill, continuous education is what prepares you for the unexpected.

It doesn't eliminate risk, but it increases your ability to respond effectively when chaos strikes.

In the context of 9/11, the lessons were clear:

- Diversify your business relationships and markets.
- Invest in understanding different cultures and languages.
- Build resilience through preparation and adaptability.

THE TAKEAWAY

Education is the engine that drives success in the Money Game. To keep moving forward, you need to:

- Commit to lifelong learning.
- Focus on practical knowledge that improves your financial literacy, cultural intelligence, and personal skills.
- Learn from your mistakes and use them as stepping stones to success.
- Embrace interdisciplinary learning—sometimes the most profound insights come from combining fields like economics and psychology.
- Step outside your comfort zone—whether it's traveling to a new country, tackling a new challenge, or learning a new language.

Remember: The rules of the game are always changing. The more you educate yourself, the better equipped you'll be to adapt, thrive, and win.

CHAPTER TEN

Artificial Intelligence – A Double-Edged Sword

WHAT IS AI AND WHY DOES IT MATTER?

At its core, AI refers to machines and algorithms that can analyze data, learn from it, and make decisions. In the world of personal finance, AI is already playing a significant role:

- Investment platforms use AI to create personalized portfolios.
- Chatbots provide financial advice and customer support.
- Algorithms detect fraudulent activity in your accounts.

AI matters because it can process vast amounts of data far faster than any human, uncovering insights that might take us years to discover. But just like a calculator doesn't replace basic math skills, AI shouldn't replace your critical thinking.

HOW AI CAN HELP YOU WIN THE MONEY GAME

1] Personalized Financial Planning

Many AI-powered tools, like robo-advisors, can help you create a financial plan tailored to your goals, risk tolerance, and timeline.

Apps like;

- Betterment, Wealthfront, and Vanguard Digital Advisor use AI to build and manage portfolios with minimal fees.
- AI tools can analyze your spending habits and suggest ways to save or cut unnecessary expenses.

Key Tip: Use AI tools to supplement your financial knowledge—not replace it. Always double-check their advice.

2) **Automating Investments and Savings**

AI can take the guesswork out of investing by automatically rebalancing your portfolio, reinvesting dividends, or adjusting your asset allocation based on market trends.

Key Tip: Automation is a great way to stay disciplined, but be sure to monitor your investments periodically.

3) **Fraud Detection and Security**

AI algorithms are excellent at spotting unusual patterns in your financial transactions, helping to protect you from fraud.

Key Tip: While AI enhances security, you should still regularly review your statements and stay vigilant about scams.

5) **Predictive Analytics for Market Trends**

Advanced AI platforms can analyze market data in real time, providing insights into trends, risks, and opportunities.

Key Tip: Be cautious with AI-generated predictions. No algorithm can guarantee market success.

THE DANGERS OF AI

1) **Over-Reliance**

It's tempting to let AI do all the thinking for you, but that's a risky strategy. AI tools are only as good as the data they analyze, and they can't account for every nuance of your personal situation or market conditions.

Example: During a market downturn, AI might recommend selling certain assets to minimize losses. However, a long-term investor may know staying the course is often the better strategy.

2] **Bias in Algorithms**

AI systems are created by humans, and they can inherit biases from their developers or the data they're trained on. This can lead to skewed recommendations or unfair practices.

Key Tip: Question the logic behind AI recommendations. Don't assume they're infallible.

3] **Privacy Concerns**

Many AI tools require access to your personal and financial data. While most companies have robust security measures, data breaches are always a possibility.

Key Tip: Only use trusted platforms and regularly review their privacy policies.

4] **Misinformation and Scams**

As AI becomes more accessible, it's also being weaponized by scammers. AI-generated content, such as deepfake videos or fake financial advice, can be incredibly convincing.

Key Tip: Always verify the source of any financial advice or information. If it seems too good to be true, it probably is.

HOW TO USE AI WISELY

1] **Stay Informed**

Understand the limitations of AI and stay updated on advancements in the technology. Knowledge is your best defense against over-reliance or manipulation.

2) **Combine AI with Human Judgment**

Use AI as a tool, not a crutch. Always apply your critical thinking and personal knowledge to any advice or insights it provides.

3) **Diversify Your Tools**

Don't rely on a single AI platform for all your financial needs. Use multiple tools to cross-check advice and ensure you're getting a well-rounded perspective.

4) **Set Boundaries**

Be mindful of how much access you're giving AI tools to your data and financial accounts. Protect your privacy by using trusted platforms and enabling two-factor authentication.

A PERSONAL ANECDOTE: WHEN TECHNOLOGY WENT TOO FAR

I remember the first time I used an AI-powered robo-advisor. It seemed like magic—an app that could build and manage a portfolio for me? Sign me up.

But over time, I started noticing some odd recommendations; like selling assets at a loss to rebalance my portfolio. The app didn't understand my long-term goals or the fact I was comfortable with some short-term volatility.

That experience taught me to treat AI tools with a healthy dose of skepticism. While they're great for automating tasks and analyzing data, they don't know me as well as I know myself. AI is a tool—not a replacement for common sense.

THE TAKEAWAY

AI is one of the most powerful tools in the Money Game, but it's a double-edged sword. To make AI your ally:

- Use it to automate, analyze, and optimize—but never stop thinking for yourself.
- Question the recommendations and always verify the logic behind them.

- Protect your privacy and stay vigilant against scams and misinformation.
- Combine the strengths of AI with your own knowledge and judgment to make smarter financial decisions.

Remember: AI can give you an edge, but the ultimate responsibility for your financial success rests with you. The best strategy is to use technology as a partner, not a master.

CONCLUSION: MASTERING THE MONEY GAME

Congratulations!

You've made it to the end of this book—a journey through the intricate, sometimes chaotic, but always fascinating, Money Game.

By now, you should have a clearer understanding of the rules, the traps to avoid, and the tools you can use to play this game smarter and with greater confidence.

But before we close, let's reflect on some of the key takeaways and the mindset that will help you not just survive, but thrive, in this game.

1. THE RULES ARE HIDDEN, BUT THEY'RE NOT IMPOSSIBLE TO LEARN

If there's one thing I've emphasized, it's that the rules of money are not always obvious. They're subtle, often obscured by marketing, societal norms, and personal habits. But they're there, and once you recognize them, you can start playing on your terms.

From understanding entropy to questioning whether every dollar spent is moving you closer to or further from your goals, knowing these rules gives you the power to make better decisions.

2. OWNERSHIP AND RESPONSIBILITY ARE EVERYTHING

Blaming external factors—whether it's the government, your upbringing, or bad luck—gets you nowhere. Taking ownership of your decisions and your goals is the cornerstone of success. Remember the squirrel analogy: work with what you've got, focus on what you can control, and prepare for the inevitable winters of life.

3. MONEY IS A TOOL, NOT THE GOAL

As tempting as it is to focus solely on earning more money, it's crucial to remember money is just a means to an end. Whether your goal is financial freedom, security, or leaving a legacy, money is the tool that helps you get there. Use it wisely, grow it diligently, and let it work for you instead of the other way around.

4. TIME, ENERGY, AND RELATIONSHIPS ARE JUST AS IMPOR-TANT AS MONEY

It's easy to fall into the trap of focusing exclusively on finances, but success is about balance. Time and energy are finite resources, and how you spend them matters just as much—if not more—than how you spend your money. Surround yourself with like-minded people who share your values and goals. These relationships will amplify your success and make the journey more rewarding.

5. LUCK FAVORS THE PREPARED

Luck is an unpredictable force, but it's not entirely out of your hands. The more you educate yourself, plan ahead, and take calculated risks, the more likely you are to be in the right place at the right time. And when bad luck strikes, as it inevitably will, your preparation and adaptability will determine how well you recover.

6. TECHNOLOGY IS A TOOL, NOT A MASTER

We live in an era where technology can either supercharge your financial journey or derail it completely. Use AI, apps, and automation to your advantage, but always stay in control. Critical thinking and personal judgment are irreplaceable.

7. PLAY THE LONG GAME

Success rarely happens overnight. It's the result of consistent effort, smart decisions, and a willingness to learn from setbacks. Set your goals, create a plan, and celebrate every small victory along the way.

Remember: the hardest choices are often the right ones, and the easiest choices often lead you astray.

A FINAL ANECDOTE: THE LONG ROAD TO FREEDOM

When I first started my business, I thought success would mean never having to worry about money again.

Over the years, I've realized that true success is about freedom—freedom to make your own schedule, pursue your passions, and enjoy the journey.

My wife and I often sit in bed in the mornings, sipping coffee, playing Wordle, and revisiting our long-term goals.

That's what success looks like to me—building a life where time, energy, and money are working together in harmony.

THE LAST RULE: NEVER STOP LEARNING

The Money Game is always changing.

Markets evolve, economies shift, and new technologies emerge. The only way to stay ahead is to keep learning, keep questioning, and keep adapting. Treat every setback as a lesson, every decision as an opportunity, and every success as a step closer to your goals.

Remember: this is your game to play. The rules may not always seem fair, but they're not impossible to master. With the right mindset, tools, and strategies, you can win—and enjoy the process along the way.

So, what's your next move?

ARE YOU WINNING THE MONEY GAME?

Reading about the rules of money is one thing, but knowing how you're applying them in your own life? That's a game-changer.

To help you assess where you stand, we've created an interactive tool: The Money Game Quiz.

This quiz is designed to give you a clear picture of how well you're playing the Money Game—and where you might be falling behind.

It only takes a few minutes to complete, and you'll walk away with actionable insights tailored to your financial habits.

Once you know your score, you'll see how well you understand the rules of the money game—or if you're getting played. Do you want to be a player or a playee? The choice is yours.

To take the quiz visit our website: www.springwellpublishing.com or scan this QR code:

Discover the Silent Strength of Quiet Money

Congratulations on mastering *The Money Game*. Now, explore the power of *Quiet Money*—the art of growing and sustaining wealth with intention. In a world of flashy, amplified lifestyles, true wealth whispers. It's the small, deliberate choices—like driving a modest car or choosing a practical home—that build lasting security and freedom. *Quiet Money* prioritizes financial growth over appearances. This isn't about sacrifice but smarter living. By letting your money grow silently, you achieve financial freedom and peace of mind. Discover how the wealthiest thrive by living below their means, leveraging discreet investments, and embracing cost-consciousness without compromise. With *Quiet Money*, you'll build a life rich in options, free from financial stress.

ACKNOWLEDGMENTS

First and foremost, I extend my deepest gratitude to my wonderful and patient wife, Alice, whose undying support and love have been my anchor and inspiration throughout the creation of "The Money Game."

Alice, your unwavering encouragement and the countless ways you assist me daily have been pivotal in this endeavor. This journey of exploring and elucidating complex financial concepts would not have been as enriching or achievable without you by my side. I must also express my appreciation for the array of online tools that have significantly enhanced my research and writing process.

These digital resources have been indispensable, not only for drafting and refining this manuscript, but also for connecting with talented individuals such as the voice actors who brought the audio version of this book to life, and the editors and proofreaders who polished the text to perfection. The availability and accessibility of such tools have truly transformed the creative landscape for writers everywhere. Lastly, I wish to acknowledge the assistance provided by ChatGPT.

Its role in helping me refine ideas, clarify financial principles, and even navigate the complexities of narrative structure has been invaluable. Its help has been a vital part of this project, and for that, I am incredibly grateful.

To everyone who has contributed, whether mentioned here by name or remembered in spirit, thank you for helping transform "The Money Game" from a concept into a reality that I hope will enlighten and inspire many.

WE'D LOVE TO HEAR YOUR THOUGHTS!

If you have enjoyed reading this book or have any feedback, we'd greatly appreciate your review on Amazon. As a new author your feedback is incredibly important and very much appreciated. Thank you for your support and for helping to spread the word!

Please scan the QR code below to leave a review.

ABOUT THE AUTHOR

Mark Hallink and his wife, Alice, are "trailblazers" in the world of Cowboy Mounted Shooting and dedicated advocates for the sport. As the first man and woman in Canada to achieve Men's Level Six (M6) and Ladies' Level 6 (L6), respectively, the highest level in the discipline, Mark and Alice's accomplishments

have inspired countless enthusiasts to pursue their own riding and shooting goals. Professionally, Mark was the founder and former president of Hallink RSB Inc., a leading innovator in the tooling and packaging industry. His company played a key role in advancing technology and design in many of the products found on your grocery store shelves, setting industry standards for quality and efficiency. After selling the company in 2020, Mark transitioned into retirement, where he now focuses on his passions: writing and spending time with the love of his life, Alice, and his favorite horse, Pumpkin. Mark studied at the University of Waterloo in Canada, earning an Honours Degree in Psychology. Mark's writing spans topics like financial literacy, where he shares his expertise in business and entrepreneurship, as well as fiction, where he explores imaginative stories inspired by his experiences and love for adventure. His work reflects his belief in perseverance, financial independence, and the joy of creative expression. Mark and Alice are retiring to North Florida, where they plan to embrace the region's natural beauty, and friendly people, and continue their equestrian pursuits, exploring new adventures around the world.

BOOKS BY THIS AUTHOR

PUMPKIN'S PENNIES

In *Pumpkin's Pennies*, young readers embark on a heartwarming journey with Pumpkin as she discovers the value of hard work, saving, spending wisely, and sharing. Set in the vibrant world of Springwell Farms, the story follows Pumpkin's determination to earn her first "horsey coins," save for a warm blanket and eventually use her financial knowledge to lead her community toward prosperity.

QUIET MONEY

Quiet Money by Mark W. Hallink is a comprehensive guide to building and maintaining wealth with a focus on living a fulfilling life, aligned with personal values rather than societal expectations. The book rejects the flashy, ostentatious displays of wealth prevalent on social media and emphasizes a more intentional, humble approach to financial success.

HOW TO SPEAK TO A ROBOT

How To Speak To A Robot is your essential guide to mastering AI communication with practical tips and creative insights. This book shows us how to use AI tools like ChatGPT to foster meaningful interactions and unlock our full potential in the digital age.

Empower yourself to lead with clarity and creativity – start the conversation today!

www.ingramcontent.com/pod-product-compliance
Lightning Source LLC
Chambersburg PA
CBHW050039040726
47599CB00015B/1753